Gu[illegible]nds

Stories by David Lewis
Illustrations by Diane Matthes

SCRIPTURE UNION , 47, Marylebone Lane, London, W1M 6AX

Contents

	page
Swinging over the river	3
Gus goes to a party	23
What it means	43
More books to read	44

Swinging over the river

It was Saturday morning, and all the boys gathered together outside the old Memorial Hall.

Gus was late, as usual. He puffed as he ran down the hill. What was it about Saturday that made it different from every other day in the week? No one knew why, but they all enjoyed it!

It had rained so heavily the night before, that the river was by now very deep. Today the boys were going to swing across. One of them had a great, big rope. Someone was going to climb up into the tree on the bank, and then they would swing backwards and forwards over the river. This was the game they loved most of all.

All the boys ran down the steep hill from the Memorial Hall to the shops at the corner. It was quite safe to run down, because outside the old seed shop there were great sacks of hay and straw which people could buy for their pets. The man who owned the shop was quite willing for the boys to bounce into them, so they were never afraid of hurting themselves at the bottom.

Gus and all the boys charged down the hill as fast as they could. There were times when they went faster than the cars! At the bottom of the hill they ran smack, bang into the sacks which cushioned their bump. They rolled over, gave a little laugh and got up.

They were just about to rush away when they saw him.

Old Barney was leaning over his garden fence and he was waving to them.

'Oh, gosh,' said Mike, 'what does he want again?'

The old man shouted, 'Boys, boys, quick, here, before you go.'

'Oh bother,' groaned Joey. 'What does he want? He always wants *something.*'

All the boys, Barney, Joe, Mike and even Gus slowly walked across to where the old man was.

'What do you want, sir?' they asked, trying to be respectful.

'Give me a hand, boys, give me a hand.'

'What's up?' said Mike.

'Well, during the storm last night, a tree blew down and it's leaning up against my back door. I can't move it by myself and if you could give me a hand, I'd be grateful.'

The boys began to moan quietly to themselves. He was a very sad old man really. He had trouble with his leg. Some people said it had been gashed by a shark; some people said he'd got it caught in a washing machine. No one really knew, but he had a bad limp, and he couldn't do very much. He couldn't walk very far, and certainly couldn't dig his garden.

'Er . . . er . . . er . . . well, we are not quite sure,' said the boys, and began to make excuses.

'What about you, Mike? You're the biggest, you're the strongest. Come and give me a hand.'

'I'll do it for 5p,' said Mike.

The old man said, 'Oh no, I haven't got 5p. Joey, you're the next biggest, you come and give me a hand.'

'Sorry, Barney, but I've got to go, we've a job to do down by the river. It's flooded, I think.'

And do you know, the boys ran away without looking back. They just called and said, 'Somebody will come, Barney. They'll give you a hand.'

The old man began to look even more sad than usual. Gus stopped; he couldn't run away.

'I'll catch you up,' he said. 'Run on ahead.' And he walked back to where the old man was cutting away at his garden hedge.

'Barney, sir, please can *I* try?'

'Well, bless my soul, Gus, you're the smallest of them all! I don't know if you can, but come on, let's have a try, eh?'

'Won't I look daft,' thought Gus, 'if I can't. If I can't move it because I'm too small!'

The old man and Gus got on either side of the log; it was certainly keeping the back door closed, but it wasn't as heavy as it looked. There was some puffing and grunting and pushing and pulling, and then they heaved the log on one side and rolled it down to the end of the garden.

It lay there. They couldn't move it any further. But the point was that now the old man could go in and out of his back door.

'Oh, thank you, Gus,' said Barney. 'I couldn't have managed without you, even though you are the smallest one of all. Bless you. I'm so grateful.'

He didn't give Gus anything — not that Gus really expected anything. He turned and walked down the path and opened the gate and then raced down to the river where the boys were. By the time he reached the place where they had made the old swing, someone had climbed up into the tree and tied the rope securely, and they were all swinging backwards and forwards.

The river had really swollen, and the water was nearly at the top of the bank. As the boys swung across, they dragged their feet in the water purposely, so much so that the water splashed everywhere! They were having a great time.

When they saw Gus coming, they threw the rope across.

'Come on, Gus, it's your turn. Hang on, and swing across as best you can.'

'Come on, Tarzan,' said Joey, 'Have a go.'

Gus held the rope between his hands and then he wrapped his legs around, too. He took a little run and swung wildly, and all the boys cheered. He was going well, but he didn't quite make it! He fell 'plop' into the water, about a foot short of the bank.

The water came up to the bottom of his jumper, up to his middle. His mother wouldn't be very pleased.

The boys just laughed and laughed. They rolled in the grass and enjoyed themselves!

'Shouldn't swim without your bathing trunks, Gus,' said Joey. 'It's not good for you. Your trousers will shrink, and you will too.' And the boys went into roars of laughter again.

Gus's eyes filled with tears. He didn't actually cry; but he felt like it. He wasn't big enough and he wasn't strong enough, he wasn't even old enough: he wasn't any good at all. And come to think of it, he wasn't really very clever at school!

'Miserable, that's what I am,' thought Gus. 'I'm no good for anything!'

The boys pulled him out, and tried to dry him in the sun. He felt a bit better when his trousers dried!

There were lots of things that Gus wasn't very good at, but old Barney could think of something that Gus had done very well.

Perhaps we are not very strong or very big or even clever. But what matters is that we are the best that we can be and that we can be kind and helpful.

It's great to remember that the important thing is not what other people think of us, but what God thinks of us. Other people can only see the outside of us. But God can see what we are really like.

Gus goes to a party

Augustus Pettigrew Brown yawned and stretched. This day was going to be different, in a very special way. Usually it was difficult for Gus to get up each morning, but today he was out of bed in a flash: it was *the* day — the day he'd been looking forward to for three weeks now. It was the day of the party.

He'd had the invitation a long time ago, and all the boys and girls in the village were going, too. It was a Saturday, so they had all day free, because the party wasn't until tea-time.

Up on the hill, there lived a very rich, old lady. She lived in an enormous house with pine trees all round it, and once a year she opened the door of her house and invited all the children in for the party. Any boy or girl who lived in the district was allowed to go to the big house.

Gus was up early. He wasn't going to do a *thing* all day, just wish the whole day away. He knew what the parties were like — they were absolutely tremendous. Gus ran across to the bathroom. He washed his face and he cleaned his teeth. He was going to get ready right away. He gently pushed open his parents' bedroom door and peeped inside. They were fast asleep!

Softly Gus said, 'Mum, Mum! Where's my clean shirt?'
Gus's mother just turned over and said, 'Go back to sleep — it's early.'
Gus wandered around until everyone was awake in the house and then he asked his mother again. 'Mum!' he said. 'Please, may I get ready *now* for the party?'
'No,' said his mother. 'I know what you're like.'

'Please,' he said, 'I'll be good.'

'No,' said his mother. 'If you dress *now* for the party, and put your clean shirt and trousers on, then before lunch-time you'd be all mucked up, you'd go in the garden; you'd do *something*.'

'No, I promise you, Mummy,' said Gus. 'If you let me dress now, I'll look after myself — I'll sit down and read all day . . .'

Gus continued to nag, and nag — you know what it's like — I'm sure you nag sometimes — and at last Gus's mother said, 'Oh, all *right*! Your trousers are on the hanger in your wardrobe, and your clean shirt's on the top shelf.'

Gus dived upstairs — and he washed again! Then he put on his shirt; put on his clean trousers, and looked proudly at himself. He was as good as his word. He sat down. He read a book he liked very much, and then he fiddled with a jigsaw.

You see, there was one rule that the old lady made about her party. 'Every year,' she said, 'anyone is allowed to come, but they *must* have clean hands and a clean shirt.' Gus really found it difficult to remain clean all day. But he knew that if he got himself dirty, there would be no party for him.

The minutes of the day seemed endless, but eventually it was nearly tea-time, and Gus said 'Good-bye', and rushed out of the house. The summer was just finishing and Gus joined with the rest of the children to begin his walk up the hill. All the children were absolutely spotless — their faces shone, and their hands were clean. The girls had clean dresses and the boys *all* had clean shirts.

It was a long walk and Gus got thirsty. 'Cor,' he said, 'I'm longing for a drink as soon as I get there.'

And then he saw the hedges. The leaves were beginning to turn brown and scarlet and crimson, and there, tucked away right along the hedge, were the biggest and the juiciest blackberries that Gus had ever seen. 'Wait for me,' he said to Elizabeth, 'I want to climb up and get one.'

'Don't you dare!' said Elizabeth. 'Remember, if you get your hands dirty or your shirt stained, she'll probably send you home.'

Gus was going to be careful, and he *could* be careful when he tried. He climbed up the bank and he grabbed hold of a branch of a tree and gently he pulled himself up to where there was an *enormous* branch of blackberries, just hanging over him.

They were the biggest and the juiciest he had ever seen. He reached up and just touched the edge of one. It was so big and so ripe and squashy, he didn't pick it, he knocked it off, and the blackberry fell 'splosh', right over the front of his white shirt.

Gus's face went as white as his shirt.

He came down with an enormous purple patch right down the front of his shirt. He took out his handkerchief and spat on it and tried to rub it clean. But the smudge became larger — and worse.

'Oh!' said Gus. 'What can I do? Look at my shirt! Elizabeth! John! What can I do? I can't go home and change — there's no time. I've been *so* clean all day — it's just happened now!'

Gus discovered that his hand could just cover the splodge. 'I'll keep my hand there!' he said to the others.

They reached the big house. It was big and shiny, with lots of lawns and flower beds all round it, and there was a servant at the door.

'Come in,' the servant said in a deep voice. The children tiptoed into the house. It was *so* big and the ceilings were *so* high! And there, standing at the door to the huge dining room, was the lady. She was all in black and her hair was grey — she looked kind, yet stern at the same time, and all the children lined up before her.

To everyone she said, 'Let me see your hands.'

Mary went up and she showed her hands, spotlessly clean. 'In you go,' the lady said.

Then Michael went up, then Elizabeth. 'Let me see your hands,' said the lady. 'And the other side? — Oh, yes, you're all right.'

Then came poor old Gus. He clutched his shirt with one hand, covering the great splodge.

'Hello, Gus, are you clean? Have you kept the rules? Let me see your hands. Gus just showed his right hand.

'Well, what about the other one?' the old lady said. And quickly Gus swapped over. 'Y-e-s, but what are you hiding there? What's under your hand, what's on your shirt?'

Gus slowly took his hand away. 'Oh!' the old lady said. 'You've dirtied your shirt!'

'But I couldn't help it . . . it was . . .'

'Oh, Gus! I'm afraid you can't come in. It wouldn't be fair to all the other children who kept themselves clean. It wouldn't be fair to all those who've been very careful all day and have obeyed my wishes.'

'But, please, Miss, I can wash it off . . .' 'No, you could never wash it off. Now Gus, I'm afraid you must go home.'

'Please, Miss . . .'

'I'm sorry — those were the rules.'

Gus felt like crying. There were actually tears behind his eyes, but he wasn't going to let them come out.

Gus turned round and he walked out of the house and down the hill. It would be a *whole year* before he could go again. So much for him being stubborn. If only he had kept the rules! They weren't very hard. They might seem a bit annoying, but they weren't *hard.* Now he had to take himself all the way home, on his own while all the *other* children went into the party, and had a wonderful time.

God has made rules, too, and He expects us to keep them! I'm afraid that, if we break them, then all the good things that God has made for us — we shall not be able to have. Especially Heaven — there is nothing sinful in Heaven, nothing that is spoilt. God's heaven is lovely and good and clean, and Jesus is there, too. Nothing that is sinful can ever live near to God.

How wonderful it is that Jesus came to this world to die on the cross for all the sin of the world — so that we can become as if there is no 'splodge' of sin spoiling our lives. Then God looks at us as if we are perfectly clean, because of what Jesus did for us on the cross.

More books to read

Gus and family